My Thoughts
On
The Lord's Prayer

Susan Kay Box Brunner

Table of Contents

ACKNOWLEDGMENT

The author, Susan Kay Box Brunner, wishes to thank Dr. Arvil Jones, Th. M., Ph.D., Pastor, Author, Editor, and Friend, for his labor of time, who fixed errors, and advised on the sections needing rewriting for clarity, and grammatical help, and for his knowledge of and in the Word of God, - and in helping me bring, 'My Thoughts on The Lord's Prayer', come alive.

Arvil Jones and Susan Kay Box Brunner met at a Book Expo Event and shared a display table. If you know anything about pastors they are not shy when it comes to talking. By the end of the event and listening, Susan learned that, Dr. Arvil Jones, Th. M., Ph D., is a happily-married-family-man, and quite the known author, editor, and pastor of Calvary Missionary Baptist Church. But most importantly, Susan witness his love for the Lord and found him to be a true believer in Christ.

- Dr. Arvil Jones, Th. M., PH.D.

Books:

Heavenly Places, Heavenly Places II, The Townsend Legacy,
- with[co-author Ernestine Collins].

Giving The Devil His Due, Marriage God's Way,

Poems of Inspiration

Available through the author, or online

cjones156@cinci.rr.com

[513-907-7751]

1304 Bonacker Ave.,

Hamilton, OH 45011

DEDICATION

Everyone - Everywhere: It is my desire, for man-kind to have and see the hope that's in a troublesome-world and know the mercy and grace shown only by my Lord and Saviour, Jesus Christ. As I have and am being shown.

Prayer has become my key, and in confessing my sin, and asking Him in my being, I've been forgiven. John 3:16-17, For God so loved the world that He gave His only begotten Son, that whosoever believeth in Him, should not parish, but have everlasting life. - For God sent not His Son into the world to condemn the world, but that the world through Him might be saved. For years Jesus was in my life, but now He is my life.

My Thoughts On
A Precious gift of Poetic Words,
'The Lord's Prayer'

Matthew 6: 9b-13 King James Version

INTRODUCTION

In the fall of 2008, a Godly woman who had been a pastor's wife, and had served alongside him on the mission field for four years, first in Germany, then in Austria, truly surprised me. After the death of her husband, this widow lady taught a woman's group on Sunday evenings, and led a monthly devotional outing with the ladies, in which she truly became - my hero. She's a woman of impeccable moral character who has, time and time again, proven herself to be virtuous and trustworthy. When I first met her, her name was Sandra Knudson. Since the death of her first husband, she has re-married, and is now known as Sandra Garverick. But because of our close friendship, she allows me to call her, simply - Miss Sandy.

What she asked of me was if I would consider being a helper with her to the fourth, fifth, and sixth grade boys and girls in the Sunday school hour. Wow! Her question almost took my breath away, and I must admit that what was running quickly through my mind was the comparison of our lives, and how un-alike the two of us were. But after a brief hesitation and a few moments of thought, I mustered up an unknown confidence, and with a smile on my face replied - "If you're sure of my help, the answer is, yes."

She taught these children more than the regular planned lessons. Miss Sandy explained the value in learning Bible memory work, and how it was a guide for you to use in all your life. I grew in knowledge, wisdom, and understanding right along with the class. She embarked on the books of the Bible, Psalms 23, The Beatitudes, and The Lord's Prayer. And when she explained the word "Hallowed", my life changed. You might say a seed was planted, or a spark was lit.

The term "Hallowed", as defined in the Bible Dictionary.com & Saxon & Old English, means - "To make holy, to honor as holy, consecrate, ordain." "Holy person, saint". Related: Hallowed; hallow.

In order to arrive at my personal usage of 'The Lord's Prayer,' I need for us to take a journey; we need to walk through the many things surrounding the event. However, for the record, I was blessed to birth four children and adopt two more. But this particular journey is dated between the years 2008 and 2017, I lost a son, who, unknown to either him or myself, was a victim of Diabetes. I have another son who awoke to being, 'Manic.' He had stopped taking a controlled medicine prescribed by his doctor, a medicine which kept him focused. But he didn't like the effects of the medicine, which, according to him, had taken total control of his life. And so, without seeking any medical advice on how to wean himself off the medicine slowly, he just stopped taking the medicine altogether. So when he suffered two back-to-back crushing happenings, it took their ongoing life's toll.

I also have a daughter and a granddaughter, (who I adopted as my daughter,) both of whom, within less than a month, almost died from drug overdoses. And me - I was diagnosed with what's called, "Zero Cancer", a mass waiting to explode, but still had to undergo surgery and radiation. And then the health of my husband declined. Still I found myself caring for two children under the age of three, because their mother had become sick. After my husband having a serious heart attack, he developed pneumonia, and suffered from an incurable lung disease, which finally led to his death. And as if things could not get any worse, I recently got that dreaded call - *"Sorry to inform you, but there's been a fatal accident. Your daughter is dead."*

And even more recently, in fact, less than three weeks ago, as I was headed for work early in the morning, my villas'-condo was broken into by burglars, who took several very valuable items from my place before being startled by my son. My computer, which contained all my books and booklets was taken, leaving me unable to finish a book I had started, and helpless as far as writing anything else.

Sometimes life comes at you hard and fast, and decisions have to be made. But was I to crash and burn, or could I be uplifted by the One who wrote on my heart while I was yet in my mother's womb? Well, words to anyone would not begin to express my indwelling thoughts of shame or fear. But the words of Christ came over and over - I will not leave you or forsake you. And then I remembered those beloved words – neither death, nor life, nor angels, nor principalities, nor powers, nor things present, nor things to come, nor height, nor depth, nor any other creature, shall be able to separate us from the love of God, which is in Christ Jesus our Lord (Romans 8:38,39). These were indeed sweet words of comfort, words which God knew I desperately needed.

During these times I sought out knowledge, wisdom, and understanding. I began by just reciting The Lord's Prayer every morning, and then again after my personal devotional, and again at night. I began meditating on the words and their meanings. What was the prayer really about, and for whom was it spoken or written? Searching brought on a form of spiritual peace and inward joy, and yet I struggled with the warfare of my own humanity that lay deep within. Reality and its gritty circumstances, situations, family issues, outside influences, didn't have quite the same hold over me anymore. Although I didn't lock myself behind closed doors, neither did I confide much in anyone about things or happenings that hovered over me or pertained to my family life.

I crept into my small devotional group meetings with that inward dread that I was going to receive that – "*I'm better than you*" attitude from the other ladies, but strangely, I received genuine support from all of them. And then I buried myself in my writings as an author of "*realistic fiction*". But that's another story, and I'll make just a brief reference. I was in an automobile accident (not my fault,) which resulted in the loss of most of my memory for thirty years. And then, in or about December of 2012, as the result of God's grace and mercy, my memory was restored.

Chapter One

Our blessed Lord, in His own inimitable manner, responds graciously to the requests of His followers. We do not know the name of the disciple who made this request – "*Lord, teach us to pray, as John also taught his disciples*", (Luke 11:1) but whoever he was, it is evident that his request was on behalf of the whole group of disciples. It is interesting, to say the least, to note that this request was made immediately after having listened to the Lord Himself praying. I have no doubt that in answering their request – "*Lord, teach us to pray*", He gave them even more than what they asked or expected from Him, and He did it in as few words as were needed. This prayer has almost universally become known and accepted as "The Lord's Prayer", and has been memorized by countless numbers of persons around the world. Not wanting to "*split hairs*", but many teachers, preachers, and others have reminded their students and peers that this prayer should be entitled "The Model Prayer", instead of "The Lord's Prayer". For the sake of this small study, let's call it "*The Lord's Model for Prayer*". According to Him, this is "*how*" the disciples, and others, should pray. Some folks take the Lord's words so literally that each time they pray, they recite this prayer verbatim. And while there is nothing intrinsically wrong with that, it was not the Lord's intention. He was teaching them "*how*" to pray, not "*what*" to pray.

We can almost see our Lord, rising up from prayer, and seeing the expressions on the faces of His disciples. The prayer He prayed before giving them this *"model for prayer"* must have captivated them. To hear the Son of God praying, engaging in holy conversation with His Father must have held them spellbound. That prayer must have been so endearing to their hearts that there was only one thing they could say when He rose from prayer – *"Lord, teach us to pray"*. No doubt these men had prayed before, and no doubt they had heard others pray. It is evident from the request itself that they had heard John the Baptist praying, and teaching his own disciples to pray, but I doubt that they had ever heard anyone pray as earnestly, as sincerely, or as intimately as this man. It was His prayer which moved the heart of the one disciple to ask on behalf of himself, and the others – *"Lord, teach us to pray"*. A young boy, after hearing his grandfather praying on his knees in the plowed ground, knelt beside his aged grandfather, saying – *"Grandpa, I wish I could pray like you."* This is what they wanted – to learn to pray as He prayed. After hearing Him pray, they understood that, compared to Him, they knew very little about the art of prayer, but wanted to become His apprentices, taught by the One who was, and still is, the Master of the art.

What a noble aspiration on the part of these men, to desire to know how to pray. The first step in learning anything that is worth the learning is to acknowledge that we don't know how to do it. If only all of us who would aspire to preach would first aspire to learn the art of prayer! These men were destined to change the course of history through their preaching, teaching and writing, but not until they first learned how to pray. How true are the words from the old hymn – Oh what peace we often forfeit, Oh what needless pain we bear, all because we do not carry everything to God in prayer. Not until we trade time for eternity will we know the full value and effects of this matchless God-given privilege of communication with our Heavenly Father. The records we have of the greatest soul-winners of all time, all, without exception, declare their dependence upon prayer for their power to preach. Every sermon our Lord has ever blessed to the salvation of any soul was wrought through agonizing prayer. And those anointed preachers of the past, who were wise enough to know that prayer must precede preaching all agree that they dared not enter the pulpit without asking for the additional prayers of the dear saints of the church. Knowing that prayer is such a powerful and effective necessity for powerful and effective preaching, the devil will stop at nothing to prevent or hinder the praying, for the preaching is only as good as the praying which precedes it.

Every temptation and trial these men were about to face demanded that they be prepared beforehand, not with swords and staves, but with the Word of God, and prayer. In asking Him to teach them to pray, they must have realized that before claiming His promise to bless and honor their preaching, they would first have to claim His promise to bless and answer their prayers. May the writer be so audacious as to propose – any preaching which is not preceded by prayer is not preaching – it is vain jangling, sounding brass, and a tinkling cymbal. The last words of the first Christian martyr – Stephen, were a prayer – Lord Jesus, receive my spirit. And - Lord, lay not this sin to their charge (Acts 7:60). How noble indeed, then, to ask – *"Lord, teach us to pray"*.

What is our hope of ever being or doing anything of eternal value to our Master if we do not learn the spiritual art of prayer? Can two walk together except they be agreed (Amos 3:3)? There is no other avenue that leads to His throne than the avenue of prayer, and it is through prayer that we come into agreement with Him concerning what to do or say. Therefore, if we have not prayed, we are not in agreement with Him, and if we are not in agreement with Him, we cannot walk with Him.

He that goeth forth and weepeth, bearing precious seed, shall doubtless come again with rejoicing, bringing his sheaves with him (Psalm 126:6). This verse I recall my mother quoting as I was a child and a wall-plaque of these words hung in our home. She gave lou as to this being her church's class, *Willing-Workers,* key verse.

Never has there been a harvest of souls that did not begin with the watering of the tears of the one who went forth bearing the precious seed. His weeping is the outward expression of his inner agony for a plenteous harvest – he is weeping as he goes, and praying as he sows. He weeps with every step he has gone, and prays for every seed he has sown. He dares not take the harvest for granted, and neither does he dare depend upon his own strength and skill. He must pray to the Lord of the harvest. He must acknowledge that he cannot make the rain to fall upon the field, and so he asks the One who can to do it for him. After he has sown, he cannot cause the blade to appear, and so he prays. And when the blade appears he cannot make it become a stalk, and he prays again. He yet sees no ear of corn upon the stalk, and he prays again. And finally, after much weeping and praying, the time of harvest arrives. He sees his family gathering around his table, hungry for the sweet corn. He rejoices as he lays the ripened corn before his family, thanking the Lord for the bountiful harvest. And so it is with the preacher of the Gospel. If the precious Word which he is to scatter has not been watered with his own tears, with much prayer, he sows in vain.

Chapter Two

After this manner therefore pray ye: Our Father which art in heaven, Hallowed be thy name. Thy kingdom come. Thy will be done in earth, as it is in heaven. Give us this day our daily bread. And forgive us our debts, as we forgive our debtors. And lead us not into temptation, but deliver us from evil: For thine is the kingdom, and the power, and the glory forever, Amen (Matthew 6:9b-13).

Did our Lord ever say a prayer for Himself alone? The question answers itself. As He is our example in all other things, so must He be our example in prayer. Not a selfish request ever fell from His lips, because no selfish thought ever made its way into His heart. We are not born with this tendency, and neither are we prone to this practice – *selflessness.* If we ever obtain it, it must be taught by another who has learned it, and once we have grasped the precept, we must practice the principle – *selflessness.* Any prayer which is prayed for self alone, which includes no one but ourselves, is a lot like the preaching which is not first tempered with prayer – it is vain, hollow, and without substance. He is *our* Father, not just *my* Father.

Our Father which art in heaven, Hallowed be thy name. Thy kingdom come. Thy will be done in earth as it is in heaven. A prayer that is worth the praying must first acknowledge

His person, *His place*, and *His possessions* - *Who He is, Where He is*, and *What He owns.* He is the Father of Abraham, Isaac and Jacob, and he is my Father, both by creation and redemption. I belong to Him as His creature, and I belong to Him as His child. He is the Father of every star in the heavens, and if another star is being born at this moment, He is the Father of that one also, for it did not form itself from nothing, but sprang from something else which He created before. And if there is one thing that men have discovered, it is that they cannot discover all that He is, nor all that He has done. He is the Father of all living and non-living things in any and all kingdoms or species into which men may divide them. He is called the Father of mercies, for He delights in mercy more than in judgment. If men have fancied that they have discovered something new under the sun – a new species of vertebrate or invertebrate, a new sea creature or earth mammal, let them not puff up with pride, for whatever they have found must necessarily have come from something He created in the beginning. Man's science has not yet caught up with the wisdom of our Father, and neither will it ever catch up, for His wisdom is as infinite as it is eternal. Every *"new"* discovery in which mortal men rejoice only broadens the scope of their own ignorance, and displays more of the infinite wisdom of our heavenly Father. However long the history of the Universe may be, whether it be millions of years, or a few thousand, man is limited as to how much he can learn. There are immeasurable distances in the heavens to which neither man's telescopes nor his mind can reach, because the sovereign will of our heavenly Father has set a boundary, beyond which mortals cannot pass.

In acknowledging *Who He is, Where He is, and What He owns*, we are humbled, and rightly so, for as there are depths within our own planet to which men in their natural state cannot descend, how much less are they able to ascend to the heights of His throne in Heaven. In 1969 men around the globe rejoiced when the first mortal set foot on the moon – an object which is a mere 238,900 miles from earth. But the yearning hearts of men are never satisfied with conquering such meager distances – they feel they must go farther, and farther, and farther still, until they are certain they have reached the utmost limit of outer space. But the farther they go, the more they are humbled, when the *discoveries of their instruments* become the *discovery of their ignorance*. Search as they may, men have yet failed to discover either the origin or the limit of time, space, and life. And so they offer their best guess to other men, hoping other men will believe them. How humbling, and yet how sweet to simply open the pages of God's Holy Word, and discover the answer which has eluded the greatest minds of all time, and yet has blessed the mind and heart of the simplest child who has prayed – Our Father which art in heaven. How humbling, and yet how sweet to know that even though our Father in heaven has denied mortal men access to His person, His place or His possessions by means of the telescope or spaceship, He has granted access to His person, His place, and His possessions by way of the Cross. His possessions, specifically named, and yet all-encompassing in this model prayer, are His name, His kingdom, His will, His power, and His glory. When we pray – Hallowed be thy name, we do not, because we cannot, to any degree make His name more Hallowed than it has ever been; we are simply acknowledging that He possesses a name that is above all others. The ancient Hebrews held His name in such reverence and honor they dared not speak it or spell it in its fullness, for fear of misspeaking or mispronouncing it, and thus dishonoring it. It is His name by possession; a name at which the devil and all his lesser devils tremble when they hear it or think of it. It is a name which He owns, and a name which, to the exclusion of all other names, declares His ownership of all things.

So magnificent and all encompassing is His name that in order for the finite minds of fallen men to have any understanding of that name, He inspired certain men to write several different aspects of His name: When He would have us know that He is the mighty God, strong and prominent, He calls Himself El, Eloah (Psalm 139:19). When He wants us to know He is the Creator, mighty and strong, He calls Himself Elohim (Genesis 17:7; Jeremiah 31:33). He is El Shaddai – God Almighty; He is Adonai – Lord; He is Yahweh/Jehovah – LORD; He is Yahweh Jireh – my provision; He is Yahweh Rapha – my healing; He is Yahweh Nissi – my banner; He is Yahweh M'Kaddesh – who sanctifies; He is Yahweh Shalom – my peace; He is Yahweh Elohim – LORD God, Lord of lords; He is Yahweh Tsidkenu – our righteousness; He is Yahweh Rohi – our shepherd; He is Yahweh Shammah – the Lord is there; He is Yahweh Sabaoth – Lord of hosts; He is El Elyon – the Most high; He is El Roi – God of seeing; He is El Olam – Everlasting God; He is El Gibhor – the Mighty God, *and He is Jesus* – the name before which every knee shall bow, and every tongue shall confess that He is Lord, to the glory of God the Father –

Look unto me, and be ye saved, all the ends of the earth: for I am God, and there is none else. I have sworn by myself, the word is gone out of my mouth in righteousness, and shall not return, That unto me every knee shall bow, every tongue shall swear (Isaiah 45:22-23). Compare these two verses with –

Wherefore God also hath highly exalted him, and given him a name which is above every name: That at the name of Jesus every knee should bow, of things in heaven, and things in earth, and things under the earth; And that every tongue should confess that Jesus Christ is Lord, to the glory of God the Father (Philippians 2:9-11).

In this model prayer, by which He is teaching them to pray, He tells them (and us) of a kingdom – a kingdom of which He is the Creator, Owner, and Monarch. It is a kingdom for which they, and us, are to pray for its coming. This means, of course, that in its state at the time He spoke of it, that kingdom had not yet come in its fullness. If His kingdom had already come in its fullness, He would not have instructed them to pray for it to come. And this, of course, means that there is a future state of His kingdom. In praying for His kingdom to come, we are coming into agreement with the Old Testament prophets, who prophesied of a coming kingdom –

But in the last days it shall come to pass, that the mountain of the house of the Lord shall be established in the top of the mountains, and it shall be exalted above the hills; and people shall flow unto it. And many nations shall come, and say, Come, and let us go up to the mountain of the Lord, and to the house of the God of Jacob; and he will teach us of his ways, and we will walk in his paths: for the law shall go forth of Zion, and the word of the Lord from Jerusalem. And he shall judge among many people, and rebuke strong nations afar off: and they shall beat their swords into plowshares, and their spears into pruning hooks: nation shall not lift up sword against nation, neither shall they learn war anymore. But they shall sit every man under his vine and under his fig tree; and none shall make them afraid: for the mouth of the Lord of hosts hath spoken it (Micah 4:1-5).

In its present state, precious souls are being added to His kingdom, and will continue to be added until He, according to His promise, has multiplied the seed of Abraham as the stars of the sky in multitude, and as the sand which is by the seashore, innumerable. In its future state, His kingdom will encompass all the redeemed of all ages, from every kindred, nation, tribe and tongue, when all earthly powers and kingdoms shall become His for eternity.

In this model prayer, by which He is teaching them, and us, to pray, He tells us of His will – a will for which we are to pray that it be done in earth, even as it is in heaven. This means, of course, that His will, at the time He spoke these words, was not being done in earth as it was being done in heaven. Even as His kingdom had not fully come, neither was His will being fully done. We are to pray that His will be done – in earth, as it is in heaven. How comforting, and yet how humbling to know that there is a place where His will is carried out quickly, and without question. Glorious and innumerous angels, who are mightier and wiser than men, hurry to do His bidding in heaven. Let us pray that we, and all men, women, and children of earth may soon learn and love to do His bidding as quickly and unquestionably as do the angels. Let us pray that His will be done in government, from the White House to City Hall. Let us pray that His will be done in schools, in families, and in churches. But first, let us pray that His will be done is us, individually.

Give us this day, or, as Luke has it – Give us day by day our daily bread. I, for one, cannot read the Word of God for very long without being convicted of some failure on my part. I have bread enough, and to spare, but thankfully, I know from whence it came. I was not the farmer who sowed the seed from which the wheat grew to make my daily bread, and I pray that the farmer who sowed that seed knew that it was not he who made the wheat to grow, but our Father which is in heaven. It is likely that I would have had my daily bread today even if I had not prayed for Him to give it to me. But if I am so ungrateful as to continue to consume what He has given, and never thank Him for it, nor ask Him for another day's supply, it is even more likely that the supply will dwindle, and eventually disappear. When we pray for our daily bread, we should remember we are praying to the One who feeds the sparrow – day by day.

And lest I should ever imagine that I am worth more to Him than anyone else, I cannot help but recall His words –
Are not two sparrows sold for a farthing? And one of them shall not fall to the ground without your Father. But the very hairs of your head are all numbered. Fear ye not therefore, ye are of more value than many sparrows (Matthew 10:29-31).

I am of more value than many sparrows – but how many? Are we glad, or are we sad, that our Lord compared our value to an un-named number of one of the smallest and most insignificant of all birds? Would we be happier if He had compared our value to a certain number of more valuable creatures? If you would know at what value any man estimates himself, ask him how many sparrows he is worth!

If only the world could understand the depth of meaning in these seven simple words – *"give us this day our daily bread"!* But having gone through all the things I have experienced personally as a believer in Christ, I can see how an unbeliever might ignore the words of our Lord, for he does not know my Lord and His provision as I do. In the loss of a husband, a son, a daughter, a granddaughter, my career, a house, and more recently my personal belongings at the hand of thieves, in all of this, I sometimes wondered where the next meal was going to come from. But my gracious Heavenly Father never once failed to provide me with food, clothing, and shelter – the bare necessities of life. He has dealt with me as an individual who needed to be taught the meaning of His words – *give us this day our daily bread.* When you have no idea from what source your daily bread is going to come, He shows you in ways you cannot fail to comprehend – He is that Source from whom all blessings flow. He is the Source of my life; in Him I live and move, and have my being. He is the Source of my strength; He is the Source of my knowledge; He is the Source of my joy; He is the source of my salvation, and He is the Source of my daily bread.

The poor widow of Sarepta had only enough meal and oil for one last serving, and was expecting herself and her son to die soon after eating it. But our heavenly Father, using the prophet Elijah as his instrument, bade her feed the prophet instead of herself and her son. By faith she obeyed the voice of the man of God. God honored her faith. I cannot believe that God multiplied the meal and oil to the full capacity of the barrel and the cruse – I rather believe He created a new supply each day, day-by-day, for as long as the drought continued. If I will but ask in prayer, He will not suffer me to hunger or thirst, but will give a fresh supply, day by day. May I ask – Would it not be presumptuous of me to ask for more than a day's supply? I believe it would be presumptuous, because to ask for more than a day's supply is to presume that there will be another day. We are not promised tomorrow's bread, for we are not promised tomorrow. As our blessed Lord instructed – Take therefore no thought for the morrow: for the morrow shall take thought for the things of itself. Sufficient unto the day is the evil thereof (Matthew 6:34).

And forgive us our debts, as we forgive our debtors. Luke has it – And forgive us our sins; for we also forgive every one that is indebted to us. *An unforgiving heart* is *an unforgiven heart*. It cannot be otherwise. The laws of God are fixed laws, and cannot be circumvented by mortals. We either forgive, or we remain un-forgiven. Though my brother sin against me seventy times seven each day, every day, if he repents, I must forgive him, and not with words only, but from my heart I must cancel all that debt. I must cancel it, and not merely cover it over for a while, and issue a new demand for payment at some future date. Forgiving others costs us nothing but our pride, and we can all afford to lose some of that. But for Christ to forgive us cost Him more than we can ever calculate. To forgive us of our sins, He made Himself guilty of our sins, and bore the ultimate penalty of His own life on a Cross. With this in mind, we should never hesitate to forgive others, no matter how great or how many the offenses they have committed against us.

And lead us not into temptation; but deliver us from evil. Can we imagine the varied reactions of the disciples as they heard Him speak all these words? Three of these disciples – Peter, James, and John, were destined to go with Him into the Garden of Gethsemane, where He would pray in an agony so intense His inner blood vessels would burst. His blood, oozing through the pores of His skin, would mingle with His sweat, and fall to the ground in great drops. Three times He would withdraw from them, agonizing alone while they slept. But do we remember what He said to them the first time He came to them after falling on His face in prayer? Simon, could you not watch with me one hour? Why sleep ye? Rise and pray, lest ye enter into temptation.

In this model for prayer, He was granting them the request – "*Lord, teach us to pray*". But from their behavior in Gethsemane, apparently they had either forgotten or simply neglected His teaching. In the model prayer, He taught them to pray – lead us not into temptation, but deliver us from evil. Our Lord, better than anyone else, knows that one step away from the corner of the street called Temptation lies the serpent called Evil, coiled, and ready to strike. It is not our will power that will ultimately conquer temptation - it is prayer, much prayer. We pray that we will not be led into temptation, but if it comes, and we are prepared through prayer, we will be delivered from the evil, because we resisted the temptation.

But let us never misinterpret our Lord's instructive words in this prayer. If we take His words literally at this point, we would be asking the Father not to lead us into temptation. Our heavenly Father will never lead one of His children into temptation. Therefore it would never be necessary for us to ask Him not to lead us there. The Apostle James makes it abundantly clear that if and when the *temptation to sin* comes, God Himself has nothing to do with the temptation:

Let no man say when he is tempted, I am tempted of God: for God cannot be tempted with evil, neither tempteth he any man: But every man is tempted, when he is drawn away of his own lust, and enticed. Then when lust hath conceived, it bringeth for sin: and sin, when it is finished, bringeth for death (James 1:13-15).

And – There hath no temptation taken you but such as is common to man: but God is faithful, who will not suffer (permit) you to be tempted above that ye are able; but will with the temptation also make a way to escape, that ye may be able to bear it (I Corinthians 10:13).

Here we must tread carefully and reverently. Our Lord is teaching His disciples to pray. So far in our prayer, we have acknowledged our Father's person, His place, and His possessions. We have prayed for His kingdom to come, and for His will to be done in earth as it is in heaven. We have asked for His forgiveness, assuring Him that we have first forgiven every person for every offense they have committed against us. And as far as material things, we have humbly asked for nothing more than our daily bread. But what does our Lord mean when He tells us to pray that our Father not lead us into temptation? In order to understand this, let's use an earthly illustration. What loving earthly father, knowing the dangers of temptation, would ever lead one of his children into temptation, knowing the evil nature of temptation? How much less would our loving heavenly Father lead one of His children into any temptation that might result in sin!

At our best, on our best day, we are susceptible to temptation and evil. It is not likely, and perhaps even impossible for us to spend a single day without being tempted in one way or another. But if we have begun our day in prayer, asking God for His leadership, we are far less likely to fall into something evil. My own *"interpretation"* of this particular request – lead us not into temptation, but deliver us from evil, would sound something like this – *"Lord, as You lead us today, deliver us from the evil of all temptations that are certain to come."* Our Lord *"allows"* temptations to come upon us, but He is not the one who sends them to us – He is the one who delivers us out of them.

Our blessed Lord Jesus, infinite in His being and attributes, very God of very God, Creator and Sustainer of the universe, condescended to men of low estate, taking upon Himself human nature, and all the susceptibilities that accompany that fallen nature, including temptation. He is able and willing to deliver us out of temptation, for He has allowed Himself to be subjected to it in all its forms, and to its utmost degree, for it is written of Him – Seeing then that we have a great high priest, that is passed into the heavens, Jesus the Son of God, let us hold fast our profession. For we have not an high priest which cannot be touched with the feeling of our infirmities; but was in all points tempted like as we are, yet without sin. Let us therefore come boldly unto the throne of grace, that we may obtain mercy, and find grace to help in time of need (Hebrews 4:14-16).

Every foul temptation which the devil is able to suggest to us humans was suggested to our great Intercessor. He faced them all, He fought them all, and He conquered them all. As a heavenly Father, He will withhold no good thing from His children, and delivering them from evil is only one of those countless good things. If any of us has ever been subjected to some temptation which seems insurmountable to us, and we have prayed for deliverance, and have rejoiced with exceeding joy when the deliverance came, how must our Lord rejoice in sending that deliverance to us!

I have no doubt that when the Lord Jesus was teaching His disciples how to pray, in using the plural terms – *"our"* and *"us"*, He was thinking, not only of the disciples themselves, but of their families also. And as the prayer applies to all of us, it should include our children, our grandchildren, and however many generations may follow us. When I pray – lead us not into temptation, but deliver us from evil, I think of my family, my friends, my co-workers, and my fellow believers around the world; the Pastors, Evangelists, Teachers and Missionaries from all nations.

Chapter Three

For thine is the kingdom, and the power, and the glory, forever, Amen. After having prayed for His kingdom to come in its fullness, we again acknowledge that it is *His kingdom* – it belongs to Him as its Creator and its reigning Monarch. But there are two other infinite attributes of God which we should never forget or ignore in our praying - we are to acknowledge His *power* and His *glory* before saying Amen. His power and His glory are His possessions in the same way His name, His kingdom, and His will are His possessions. There is a power which belongs to Him exclusively – no other being possesses it in exactly the same kind or degree in which He possesses it. And this exclusive power is not limited to His ability to do all that He wills to do, but it also denotes His authority over all created things. He possesses both the power and the authority to do as He pleases, when He pleases, and for as long as He pleases.

His is the power that called the universe into being, using nothing but His bare Word and Will. The power and authority of His Word and His Will is the first cause of all that exists. His is the power that created the heavens and the earth. His is the power that created man from the dust of the earth. His is the power which called forth the blades of grass, and the countless stars of the countless galaxies, all of which He called by name. His is the power that brought plagues upon the Egyptians while protecting His heritage Israel. His is the power that removed the wheels of the Egyptian chariots as they pursued His people. His is the power which opened the waters of the Red Sea for His people to pass over on dry land, and His is the power that brought the same waters in upon his enemies, drowning them all. And His is the power that raised our Lord Jesus from the dead.

One of the many irrefutable testimonies we have to the Deity of Christ Jesus is the claim He made, saying – All power is given unto me in heaven and in earth (Matthew 28:18). If, as I have stated, the power of God is an exclusive power, belonging to Him alone, and Jesus claims that power for Himself, then Jesus was claiming to be God, in flesh. And while here, in His flesh, He demonstrated that power, in His service, in His suffering, and in His salvation of men and women.

We mortals are so restricted in our ability to know our God in all His glorious attributes, but we are given glimpses of His glory in studying His Word, where we discover, little by little, the things that make Him Who He is. In studying the attributes of God, each is infinite and eternal, having no limitations, no beginning, and no end. It is therefore impossible for us who are but creatures of a moment to fully understand our God. We make puny attempts to classify anddistinguish between His attributes, only to find ourselves at a loss to find them out to the utmost.

But as some of the ancient students and scholars of the Scriptures have attested, there seem (to us) to be some attributes of God which sparkle with a bit more luster than others. As one star differs from another star in glory and brilliance, so it seems to us that one attribute of God shines a bit brighter than another. Some of the dear brethren from the past have argued — *"If there was one attribute of God which He might defend more than any other, it would likely be either His holiness or His glory."*

And since the Holy Spirit makes no mistakes, and since there is nothing in the Holy Bible that was put there by mere chance or coincidence, He chose to leave this attribute – His glory, as the last thing we are to acknowledge in our praying. We can only speculate as to why He chose to do so. In being a born-again believer, we share in His name, we share in His kingdom, and although we can never attain the same degree of power which belongs to Him exclusively, He has given us power through His Holy Spirit. And in reading His Holy Word, we are made to know, and share in His Will. We are given the privilege of sharing in some of His attributes, but not in all of His attributes. His glory, which is one of His in-communicable attributes, He will not give to another, He will not share it with another. It is a glory which necessarily, because if His nature, transcends the glory of all created things, individually and corporately.

I am the LORD: that is my name: and my glory will I not give to another, neither my praise to graven images (Isaiah 42:8). And – For mine own sake, even for mine own sake, will I do it: for how should my name be polluted? And I will not give my glory unto another (Isaiah 48:11). And – O LORD our Lord, how excellent is thy name in all the earth! Who hast set thy glory above the heavens (Psalm 8:1).

He associates His name with His glory. There is not another name more glorious, and there is no other glory as glorious as His. A mere handful of mortals have been blessed with small glimpses of His glory, including Moses, Isaiah, Job, Peter, James, and John, but none have ever beheld Him in all His glorious splendor. His is a glory from which the exalted Seraphim hide their faces and their feet, crying Holy, holy, holy is the Lord of hosts: the whole earth is full of his glory (Isaiah 6:2-3).

And while we creatures of earth pray to Him, acknowledging His person, His place, and His possessions, asking for His forgiveness, and for our daily bread, we who are His by the new birth, humbly and reverently anticipate a coming day in which we will be granted the high honor of seeing the King in all His glory. Amen.

My Questions

Do you want to have a peace that passes all understanding?
1. Are you tired of carrying life around by yourself?
2. Would you like to know an unconditional love?
3. To be forgiven and set free?
4. Are you afraid you're not good enough?
5. Have you put off waiting until another time to accept Him?

If the answer is yes to any of these questions now is the time to accept Jesus. You're not promised tomorrow. Just stop and pray where you are and ask Jesus into your life and be sincere about confessing all your sin and ask Him to come in and dwell with you. He will. Now follow His lead share your experience with others stay faithful.